The Lady
and
the Unicorn

The Lady and the Unicorn

Alain Erlande-Brandenburg

Curator

of the Cluny Museum

 Editions de la Réunion des Musées Nationaux

ISBN 2-7118-0118-7 / 8162-021
© Éditions de la Réunion des Musées Nationaux
10 rue de l'Abbaye, 75006 Paris, 1979 et 1983

The Lady
and
the Unicorn

Taste
Sight
Smell
Touch
Hearing
A mon seul désir

A study

For Gilles.

Certain masterpieces of art exercise such universal fascination that it is difficult to consider them objectively. Every detail contributes to delight the eye : the range of colouring, the disposition of the different scenes and an indefinable atmosphere of poetry. The six panels which compose the tapestry known as *The Lady and the Unicorn* fall into this category and the Cluny Museum has enhanced its fascination by exhibiting it in a round hall specially conceived so as to encircle the visitor. Each element contributes to its charm and stimulates our imagination to the utmost. The contrasting colours — the red background in striking contrast to the dark blue island — creates an almost unique impression of harmony. The decoration (inspired by leaves, flowers and trees commonly to be found in France) provides a great variety of colours : a multitude of flowers planted in the soil of the island; flowering branches scattered over the red background. Added to these, we see trees : oak, pine, holly and flowering orange-trees. Familiar animals like foxes, dogs, duck and partridge mingle with exotic lion-cubs, panthers or cheetahs. Our gaze lingers with pleasure on a fabulous beast dating from the remotest antiquity, with the body of a horse, the head of a goat and a horn which is in reality a narwhal's tooth : in other words, a unicorn. Naturally, this imaginary beast had to be credited with extraordinary powers, especially during the Middle Ages and even in our own times it is surrounded by a certain aura of mystery. The lion, on the other hand, is more familiar, though it sometimes has a disconcertingly ironical smile. To all this must be added the Lady. She appears in all six panels, each time in an ordinary, everyday attitude and dressed in a different costume and with a different headdress. A serving-maid accompanies her so as to show her by contrast tot he best advantage. Each scene created an impression of mystery and this was enhanced by the crescents decorating banners, standards, escutcheons and emblasoned capes.

The more recent history of the tapestry also made a great impression on the public. It was discovered in 1844 by the famous novelist George Sand, in the château at Boussac, an obscure little town in the department of the Creuse. Thirty-nine years later, it was acquired by the Cluny Museum where it at once became popular. Other writers sang its praises : Rilke was enthralled by it and expressed his enthusiasm in some fine verses, and Jean Cocteau was enchanted in his turn.

Historians attempting to reconstitute its history succumbed in their turn to its charm and helped to reinforce a legend which overshadows it today. Because of the presence of the young woman, it was supposed to have been commissioned as a wedding present. The constant repetition of the crescent motif suggested the fascination of the East. The combination of these two elements combined to create the legend of Prince Zizim, son of Mahomet II and brother of Bajazet, who was held prisoner in the Creuse and was supposed to have commissioned the tapestry for his lady-love. Later authors held it to be an allegory of the Blessed Virgin, while yet others believed the young woman to represent some famous personnage,

such as Margaret of York, the third wife of Charles the Bold. Each panel was interpreted according to the writer's own point of view. History, in its cold, heartless way, has destroyed most of these theories and has discovered the answer to a number of questions, though others still remain obscure.

Our desire to solve the mystery of *The Lady and the Unicorn* leads us to observe it with special attention. The eye is first of all delighted by the colouring and a sort of magic in the spectacle, then we begin to realise how amazingly different are each of the panels. Four different kinds of trees frame each of the scenes, creating a diverging perspective further emphasised by the flag-poles. The skilful composition is given its full value by the lion and the unicorn who face each other symetrically, or by the flaps of a magnificent tent, opening to reveal the young woman at its entrance. Just as striking is the beauty of the draftsmanship. One hardly knows what to admire most : the slender bodies of the women, their delicate features or the elegance of certain animals. The attitudes and gestures of the Lady and her companion are simple and familiar, yet they seem to be eternal.

Time has slightly faded the bright colours, but they bear witness to the skill and experience of the craftsmen who wove the tapestry. Brocades, velvets, silks and jewels have been rendered in wool with extraordinary exactitude.

It is only with an effort that we can manage to break free from all this enchantment and try to understand the true meaning of the work. The arms — *Gules, a Bend Azure charged with three Crescents Argent* — are those of the Le Viste's, a family from the region of Lyon, which had distinguished itself in the King's service in Paris. It has even been possible to identify its owner : Jean Le Viste, President of the Court of Aids. The continual repetition of these arms suggests a proud man in a high position, for whom the tapestry was a means of proclaiming his glory. In this case, the lion and the unicorn are simply there to act as supporters, such as are frequently seen in coats of arms.

There can be no question, however, of reducing the tapestry to this one significance. There is another, more general one, which reveals its full meaning. It is recognised today that five of the six panels illustrate the five senses, and these are easily explicable. Sight: the unicorn is watching itself in a looking-glass held out to him by the Lady. Hearing : she is playing at portable organ worked by her servant. Smell : a monkey perched on a stool is sniffing at a carnation while the Lady weaves a wreath of flowers. Taste : a monkey raises a sweetmeat to its mouth, while the young woman chooses another from a comfit-dish. Touch : here, she is shown holding the unicorn's horn very gently in her hand.

There remained the last panel, for which no satisfactory explanation had been found. It had even been supposed to belong to a different series. This hypothesis is perhaps ingenious but it unconvincing in view of the inscription on the tent : *A mon seul désir*, in conjunction with the gesture the Lady seems on the point of making. In spite of what has so often been affirmed, she is not choosing jewels from the casket held out by her maidservant, but is delicately replacing in it the necklace she has just unfastened from her neck. In other words, she is not accepting these jewels as a gift, but is laying them aside. Seen in this light, the inscription *A mon seul désir* reveals its true meaning. It should be considered as relating to the *Liberium arbitrium* of the Greek philosophers who believed that freedom from the passions provoked by ill-controlled senses would ensure right behavior. The Lady's gesture thus illustrates the inscription on the tent and the six panels of *The Lady and the Unicorn* reveal a deep moral significance.

Two problems remain unsolved : the personality of the artist who designed the tapestry for Jean Le Viste, and the place where it was woven. The style shows it to have originated within Court circles, but that is about all that can be said, since the original paint has almost entirely disappeared. As to where it was woven, there have been many suppositions, both in past and recent times, but all have been disproved by modern scholarship. The millefleurs background once suggested the hypothesis of a travelling workshop carrying on its trade along the banks of the Loire. We know now that it must have been woven in one of the Northern cities specialising in this technique. This may have been Brussels. Whatever the name of the painter may have been, or wherever it was woven, *The Lady and the Unicorn* remains one of the great masterpieces of tapestry. All the poetry of the Middle Ages, which was being driven out by a new conception of art, seems to have found a refuge in this technique.

The Lady
and the Unicorn
Sight

The face of the kneeling unicorn is reflected in the looking-glass held out by the Lady, thus clearly indicating that Sight is the sense illustrated here. The young woman wears a brocade gown turned back over the knees. The underskirt of pale blue moiré falls in numerous folds and spreads over the floor. The neckline is held in place by a double necklace joined by a clasp. As in *Hearing*, the hair is caught up in braids over the veil and twisted into a plume. The serving-maid appears neither here nor in *Touch*.

The original colouring of the unicorn has retained much of its beauty. The clearly defined shadows emphasise the elegance of the body and its articulations.

The island is very slightly tilted against the pale pink background and this produces the same reversed perspective we find in *Smell* and *Taste*.

h. 3 m 10 / l. 3 m 30

The Lady
and the Unicorn
Hearing

There can be no doubt as to the interpretation of this scene : the Lady is playing a portable organ while her maidservant works the bellows. She wears a brocade robe, slit up the side to show the blue underskirt. Long, very wide sleeves cover the silken shirt banded at the wrists. The brown veil falling over her shoulders is held in place by two braids of hair which meet high over the forehead to form an aigrette. The maidservant wears a dress of blue moiré, also with very wide sleeves, opening at the side to show a sky-blue underskirt. Her hair is care-fully combed, held back by a head-band and partly hidden by a muslin veil.

The artist has portrayed the lion and the unicorn twice, since they figure on the end-posts of the por-table organ. The perspective effect is obtained from this instrument and the table supporting it.

The red background has slightly faded with time; the pink of the banners and standards is produced by means of vertical hatchings.

h. 3 m 70 / l. 2 m 90

The Lady
and the Unicorn
Taste

The monkey at the base of the tapestry is popping a sweetmeat in his mouth, thus completing the gesture commenced by the young woman. The Lady helps herself absent-mindedly to a sweet from the comfit-dish held out by her maidservant. She is absorbed in watching a splendid parakeet which holds a sweet in its claws. The brocade gown has a long train and is slit in front to reveal her underskirt. The veil, held in place by a headband, floats gracefully in the breeze, in harmonious balance with the movement of the left hand. The maidservant too is splendidly dressed in a short-sleeved gown of blue moiré which partly conceals the long sleeves of her shirt and the brocade underskirt.

The composition, closed at the back by a semicircular wooden fence covered with climbing roses, is based, as in *Smell*, on the principle of inverted perspective.

The tapestry has retained the original freshness of its colouring : the red contrasts with the pink of the escutcheons worn by the standard bearers. The unicorn was originally tinged with gold and this colour was restored when the tapestry was recently cleaned.

h. 3 m 75 / l. 4. m 60

The Lady
and the Unicorn
Smell

The gesture of the monkey perched on his stool, provides the explanation for this panel. He is sniffing at a carnation stolen from the basket. The maiden is taking carnations from the basket held out to her by her servant and pays no attention to what is happening behind her.

The gown is of dark blue, with paler shadows obtained by hatching and is hooked back to reveal the underskirt of gold brocade. The arms are covered with sleeves of fine muslin fitted at the wrists. The belt consists of a plaited cord, revealing a tendency towards a simpler style of dress. The oval of the face

is beautifully set off by the short veil studded with precious stones which covers her hair, and by the headband holding it in place.

The maidservant wears a moiré gown on which the pattern on the Lady's gown is repeated in blue. Here too, the shadows are marked by hatching.

The effect of several different levels is obtained by the tilt of the island and by spears and bushes which create an inversed perspective converging towards the eye of the beholder.

h. 3 m 67 / l. 3 m 22

The Lady
and the Unicorn
Touch

The meaning of this scene is revealed in the gesture of the Lady. She is touching the unicorn's horn with her left hand while the right firmly grips the spear.

Her clothes are particularly splendid. The short-sleeved robe of blue-black velvet lined with ermine opens to give a glimpse of the gown of gold brocade on a dark-blue foundation. The magnificence of the costume is enhanced by her jewels : the metal belt from which hangs a long chain, a necklace composed of rings and dangling pendants, a diadem rising in a peak above the forehead. Her splendid fair hair flows loose to her waist.

The composition is extremely skilful, being based on a diagonal line starting at the animal's horn, continuing with the young woman, who is leaning slightly backward, then with the spear, before disappearing in the pine-tree. The artist has been careful not to unbalance this original composition by giving too pronounced a tilt to the island and has planted trees at its edges to form parallel lines.

The lower part of this panel was badly damaged and has been entirely restored. The original red background has faded to a sort of wine colour. Like the five other tapestries woven with threads of wool and silk, there are six threads to the centimetre.

h. 3 m 72 / l. 3 m 58

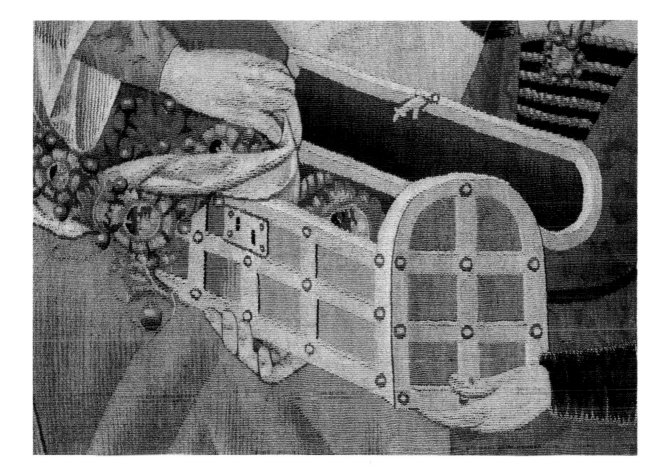

The Lady
and the Unicorn
A mon seul
désir

This last tapestry is certainly the most beautiful of all. The artist understood its deeper meaning and treated the scene with special care. It has been remarkably well preserved, except for the lowest band, which has been rewoven. The young woman wears a red gown turned up over a brocade underskirt. The sleeves fit close to the wrists and are glimpsed through transparent muslin. The hair hangs loose and is hidden by a heavy turban from which rises a slender aigrette. The maidservant wears a low-necked dress of red moiré. Her hair is caught up in braids over her forehead to terminate in an aigrette, in the style worn by the Lady in *Hearing* and *Sight*.

The important role played by this scene in the general significance of the tapestry is emphasised by the moiré tent studded with golden tear-drops, the flaps of which open to form a magnificent frame for the young woman replacing her necklace in the casket. The perspective too draws the eye of the spectator towards the central scene. The colours have retained all their original freshness, the background is still brilliant and the tear-drops stand out against the blue of the tent.

h. 3 m 78 / l. 4 m 66

The Lady
and the Unicorn
A study

The château of Boussac

I. Historical account.

The mystery with which *The Lady and the Unicorn* has been so complacently surrounded stems from legends created in the 19th century and which modern erudition finds it hard to destroy, especially since certain facts remain obscure. The present *Study* is an attempt to throw some light on a subject about which so much has been written and so many conflicting theories elaborated both in the past and in more recent times. It will also allow us to describe more fully than was possible in the *Introduction* certain theories put forward by people who have often not taken the trouble to justify them.

The « invention » of the Lady and the Unicorn

The fame of this tapestry rests first of all on the strange fact that it was, if not discovered, at least revealed to a wide public, by one of the most illustrious writers of the 19th century. George Sand saw it on several occasions at Boussac, in the home of the sub-prefect, who had his apartment and offices in the château. She was struck by its beauty and mentioned it in her novel, *Jeanne*, which first appeared in 1844. A study of the costumes had already convinced her that it dated from the end of the 15th century. She discussed the subject at greater length in an article written for *L'Illustration* in 1847 and

illustrated by her son Maurice. In 1862 she repeated some of her previous remarks in *Autour de la Table*. Finally, in 1871, she described once more, in *Journal d'un voyageur pendant la guerre*, three panels of the ensemble, seen at night by the flickering light of a candle.

It is not sure that George Sand was the first to draw attention to *The Lady and the Unicorn*. It is difficult to determine the precise date at which she saw it for the first time and she may have discovered it through her husband and son, who visited the subprefect of Boussac as early as October 1835. It was possibly then that Maurice made the drawings used to illustrate the 1847 article.

Well before that date, Prosper Merimée, then Inspector of Historic Monuments, had drawn the attention of the authorities to the beauty and importance of this work. When the Commission for Historic Monuments met in April 1842, he had suggested the State should acquire it for the sum of 3.000 francs. In July 1841, he had already written a long letter to his predecessor, Ludovic Vitet, expressing his enthusiasm for the Boussac tapestry. Thus, thanks to him, negotiations were set in motion which were to bring results forty years later.

The tapestry at Boussac

Prosper Merimée's aim had been to save the tapestries, which were already in a bad state of preservation. The château of Boussac belonged to the parish, which had bought it in 1837 from the last private owner, a descendant of the Comte de

◄ The Capture of the Unicorn, *mille-fleurs tapestry, second series, Metropolitan Museum, New-York.*

In the Salon :

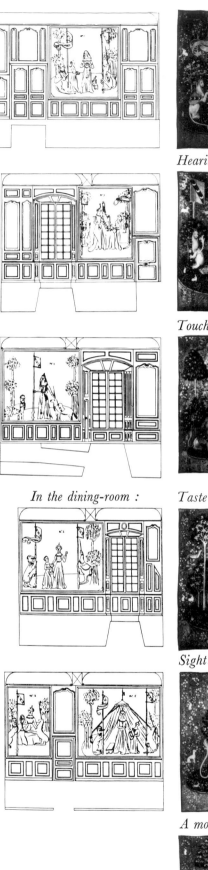

In the dining-room :

*The tapestries
at Boussac
in 1841*

Smell

Hearing

Touch

Taste

Sight

A mon seul désir

Carbonnières. The offices and apartments of the sub-prefecture were then installed there. The tapestry, considered as part of the furniture, had been included in the sale.

Thanks to previous information provided by Merimée and especially to the survey undertaken, probably at his request, by the architect Morin in September 1842, we know exactly how the tapestries were presented at Boussac. They were disposed in a décor of mid-18th century panelling, specially created for them and still in existence. *Smell, Hearing* and *Touch* were in the *Salon; Taste, Sight* and *A mon seul désir* in the dining-room. For a long time, they had been sustaining damage from the damp walls. Prosper Merimée thus proposed to the Commission that, if the State did not make this purchase, at least each panel should be isolated from the walls by a wooden frame, after being restored at Aubusson. It was calculated that 2.500 francs would be needed and a sum of 1.500 francs was allocated to help the Parish. This subsidy, however was diverted to another use and served to repair the walls of the château. The tapestries continued to deteriorate. In 1853, Baron Aucapitaine drew the attention of Edmond Du Sommerard, Curator of the Cluny Museum and a member of the Commission for Historic Monuments, to this state of affairs. At this period, the three panels which had decorated the sub-prefecture dining room, were lying, rolled up and abandoned, attacked by damp and rats, in the Town Hall of Boussac.

The tapestry at Cluny

The Commission was alerted once more, Baron Guilhermy revealed that in 1877, the town council had started negociations for the sale of the tapestry to a member of the Rothschild family residing in Vienna. Du Sommerard was sent to Boussac to offer 20.000 francs on behalf of the State. The affair was not concluded till 1882, when thc Council agreed to sell for 25.000 francs. The six panels were then deposited in the Museum of the Thermae and of Cluny which was then under the control of the Commission for Historic Monuments.

They were exhibited in a room officially inaugurated in 1883 by Jules Ferry, Minister for the Arts, and this setting, which was never really satisfactory, remained unchanged until the second World War. After the Liberation, it was decided to renovate the Museum and a new circular hall was built specially to house *The Lady and the Unicorn*. Thus isolated, its exceptional quality showed up to the best advantage.

Meanwhile, it had been restored several times. Little is known of the restoration in Aubusson mentioned by George Sand in 1847, and it was not sufficient. Between 1889 and 1894, the ferm of Lavaus carried out extensive repairs for the Cluny curators :

the base of each panel worn away by damp was rewoven with badly dyed threads, the colour of which faded rapidly. Further restoration — cleaning, rewarping and needle-darning of certain parts — was undertaken between 1941 and 1944 by the House of Brégère. Finally, in June 1975, it was recleaned, by means of the most modern techniques, which restored the original brilliance of the colours.

The first owners : the Le Viste's

It is easy to recount the recent history of *The Lady and the Unicorn*, but much harder to trace it back over the centuries. The few facts known for certain have been wrapped around like a cocoon by legends.

During the Romantic period, the presence of crescents on banners, standards and escutcheons, as well as all the shafts, gave rise to a marvellous legend of the Orient. By the beginning of the 19th century it was already believed that the tapestry had been woven for Zizim, son of Mahommed II and brother of Bajazet, when he was a prisoner at Bourganeuf. The maiden was supposed to represent his lady-love.

In 1883, Edmond Du Sommerard tore this fine story to shreds in his supplement to the catalogue of the Cluny Museum. He had recognised on the banners, standards, emblasoned capes and escutcheons the arms of Le Viste family : *gules, a bend azur, charged with three crescents argent.*

Since then, this family, which had its origins in Lyon, has been the subject of several studies concerning the problem of the tapestry's first owner. Various solutions were suggested and the affair was further complicated by the almost universally accepted belief that it had been woven for a mariage as a present to the fiancée. The presence of the maiden, repeated six times, and the scene of *A mon seul désir* — said to represent her *choosing her jewels* — gave a certain consistency to this thesis. In 1924, Henry Martin claimed that each panel portrayed Claude Le Viste, daughter of Jean Le Viste, deceased in 1500, and of Geneviève de Nanterre. This young woman had first been married to Geoffroy de Balzac, who died in 1509. The date of this first mariage is not known, but in 1513, she was remarried to Jean de Chabannes, lord of Vandenesse, brother of the famous Marshal de la Palisse. Henry Martin thought therefore that the tapestry must date from between 1509 and 1513. Just recently, in 1976, Mr Carl Nordenfalk suggested, as several others had done, that this date was too late. He rejected the Claude Le Viste hypothesis in favour of her cousin, Antoine, son of Aubert Le Viste, Jean's younger brother, who was twice married, first with Jacqueline Raguier, then with Charlotte Briçonnet. According to this theory, he commissioned *The Lady and the Unicorn* for his first wife.

Jean Le Viste

The arms depicted in the tapestry bring formal proof that this theory is false. If the tapestry had been a wedding present, the bride's arms would have been shown according to custom, on an escutcheon party per pale, with the husband's arms on the right and those of the father on the left. In reality, we see here arms « without any difference », which can only be those of a man. The hypothesis of a wedding present is thus definitively demolished. We shall see that the iconography provides a better explanation.

Thus we must return to the Le Viste family. From the region of Lyon, they spread rapidly over Burgundy, the Bourbonnais and the Ile-de-France. Like many middle-class families of the 15th century, they

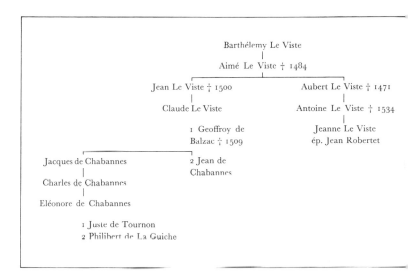

came to seek their fortune in Paris and entered the Royal Administration, where they soon distinguished themselves. Barthélemy Le Viste became Councillor to Parliament in 1440. His son Aymé succeeded him at this post in 1474, after having been councillor-clerk in 1461 and assistant to the generals of the Court of Aids in 1466. He died in 1484, leaving two sons. The elder, Jean, was appointed councillor to Parliament between 1462 and 1469. His nomination by Louis XI in 1471 as seventh master of the Court of Petitions roused a storm of protest. He was President of the Court of Aids when he died on June 1st 1500. The career of his younger brother, Aubert, who died in 1493, was less brilliant. He was not appointed councillor till February, 1492, a year before his death. Previously, he had been recorder at the Chancellery, a post he resigned in favour of his son-in-law, Jean Briçonnet. Unlike Jean, who had only one daughter, Claude, Aubert Le Viste had two children, a daughter and a son, Antoine, who was the last to bear his name since he died without male issue. With his career, the family attained its zenith : he was Recorder in ordinary to the Royal Household till 1523, when he was appointed president of the Paris Parliament. He was sent to England as ambassador-extraordinary to negociate a marriage between Louis XII and Mary of England and died full of honours in 1534.

The Cluny tapestry, commissioned by a man of the Le Viste family, may thus be attributed to Barthélemy, Aymé, Jean, Aubert or Antoine. The costumes date from the end of the 15th century and we can thus eliminate Barthélemy and probably Aymé, who died in 1484. The arms prove that it could not have been Aubert, since he died before his elder brother and never bore the full arms of his family. As for Antoine, he could not have born them till after the death of his uncle Jean in 1500, and this seems too late a date in view of the style of *The Lady and the Unicorn*. There remains Jean Le Viste.

This hypothesis is supported by another argument. When M. Pierre Verlet published an inventory, drawn up in 1595, of the château of Montaigu-le-Blin in the Bourbonnais, he noted the mention of other tapestries with a red background decorated, with arms showing the famous crescent : « Five panels of tapestry with red background, for the surrounds of a chimney-piece, on them are arms with three crescents », — « Five panels of tapestry with red backgrounds, where are sibills and unicorns with arms bearing three crescents. » « Plus another tapestry on red background where are shown unicorns and beasts with arms bearing crescents and this in seven panels... » The author of the inventory would certainly not have been able to identify the arms of a family extinguished long before, but we can recognise them at once for those of the Le Viste's. The red background, the unicorns and the animals are similitudes which lend force to the idea that, though the tapestries at Montaigu-le-Blin are not to be confused with that now at Cluny, they were of the same origin. This origin was the collection of Jean Le Viste, from which they were bequeathed to different heirs and ended up either at Montaigu-le-Blin or at Boussac.

We have seen that Claude Le Viste, Jean's only daughter married Jean de Chabannes in 1513. When she died without issue, her estate was divided between Charles de Chabannes, brother of the Marshall de la Palisse and nephew to Jean, and Jeanne, daughter of Antoine Le Viste. Charles de Chabannes had a daughter, Eléonore, whose inheritance raised certain problems. It was for this reason that an inventory was drawn up in 1595 to facilitate the division of her estate between her second husband, Philibert de la Guiche, Grand Master of Artillery, and Anne and Françoise de Tournon, daughters of her first marriage. Thus part of Jean Le Viste's personal estate arrived at Montaigu-le-Blin at the end of the 16th century.

Henry Martin has followed the history of *The Lady and the Unicorn* up to 1837. From Claude's estate it came into the possession of Jeanne Le Viste. From thence, after a series of bequests, it became the property of Jeanne de la Roche Aymon who married François de Rilhac in 1660 and brought the tapestries to her husband's château at Boussac. When Louise de Rilhac married François de Carbonnières in 1730 the château came into the possession of the latter family, where they remained till they were sold in in 1837.

The Cluny tapestries were therefore executed between 1484, when Jean Le Viste gained the right to bear the full arms of his family after his father's death, and 1500, the date of his own death. It is impossible to be more precise. We may wonder, however, in view of the pride in his arms expressed by the tapestry, whether it was not executed either when he became head of his family, or when he was appointed President of the Court of Aids in 1489. It is easy to imagine the pride Jean took in this promotion, which advertised to the world the ascension of the Le Viste's in the Royal Administration. His tomb bears witness to a glorious career, since he was buried before the high altar in the church of the Célestins in Paris, reserved in principle for great servants of the monarchy. A copper slab, stamped with his arms and showing him in his official robe, evokes his memory.

*The funeral slab of Jean Le Viste
at the Célestins in Paris,
Gaignières collection.*

II. Iconography

The mystery surrounding the history of *The Lady and the Unicorn* until quite recently, left the way open for the most extravagant speculations in the realm of iconography. We have seen that George Sand saw in it an evocation of the love of Prince Zizim for a young person from whom he was separated in his exile, or for a niece of Pierre d'Aubusson, whose prisoner he was. In 1935, Mrs Phyllis Ackerman believed the Lady to be an image of the Virgin and the unicorn a symbol of Christ. More recently, it was supposed to illustrate some unspecified doctrine of the Cathare sect. Then in 1965, Mme Lanckoronska thought she had recognised the face of Margaret of York, last wife of Charles the Bold. None of these explanations — and there have been many others — stand up to critical examination or merit refutation.

The number of tapestries.

The first question we must ask ourselves at the beginning of an iconographic study is : do the six panels form a single, homogeneous tapestry, or are they remnants of several different ensembles? There have been arguments in favour of both these theses, since testimonies from the 19th century contradict each other. In 1841, Prosper Merimée wrote to Ludovic Vitet that he had seen six tapestries on the walls of the salon and dining room at Boussac, and Morin's drawings show them there. George Sand, on the other hand, claimed in *L'Illustration* in 1847 and in *Autour de la Table* in 1862, to have seen eight. She does not mention the number in *Jeanne*, and when *Le Journal d'un Voyageur* was published in 1871, she discusses only the three in the salon. In the first two texts, George Sand says : « In the *eight* large panels filling the walls of two huge rooms, we see the portrait of a woman... » an affirmation incompatible with the testimony handed down by Morin in his drawings. That the novelist was in error becomes even more evident in her description of the different panels : in one, she recalls a young girl seated, « caressing the unicorn's horn with both hands »; she is probably thinking of *Touch*, where the Lady is standing, making indeed this gesture, but with one hand, while the other supports a standard. In another, she is said to be « seated on a richly decorated throne », which is no doubt a confusion with *A mon seul désir* (on account of the stately tent), or *Sight*, which is the only panel where she is shown seated. George Sand must have been relying here on notes taken too rapidly at the time. One is struck, moreover, by the fact that her son's drawings in the 1847 article were reversed in the process of engraving, without her noticing this. We should point out that Merimée himself was mistaken when, writing of *A mon seul désir*, he describes a young woman sitting cross-legged beneath a tent.

Nevertheless, it cannot be denied that there were other tapestries at Boussac. Several testimonies from the 19th century agree on this point in spite of their imprecision. In this letter to Ludovic Vitet, Merimée repeats what he was told by the Mayor, who claimed that several other, even more beautiful panels had been cut up by one of the Comtes de Carbonnières to cover his carts or be used as rugs. At the beginning of the present century, La Villatte, who collected several documents concerning the tapestry at Boussac, points out that certain inhabitants remembered there had been other panels besides those acquired by Cluny. Some had been used by employees of the sub-prefecture as rugs, others by the sub-prefect to protect a piano during its removal. None of these testimonies suggest the works were of the same period or the same style as *The Lady and the Unicorn* or formed part of the same series. The tapestries may have been completely different. Only one thing is certain : during the 18th century the six panels were deliberately grouped together and the *salon* and dining-room were fitted up for this purpose. This proves that they were considered at that time as forming an ensemble and their value was appreciated sufficiently to justify presenting them with great care.

The five senses

It is therefore essential to try to determine the significance of the six pictures composing *The Lady and the Unicorn*. According to the most likely hypothesis, five of them represent the five senses. Mr Kendrick has demonstrated this, and supported his thesis with a number of examples drawn from works executed in different techniques. Since then, Mrs Schneelbalg-Perelman has backed up his assertions by pointing out that an inventory drawn up in 1653 for Mazarin, mentions a tapestry depicting the five senses in much the same way as that in the Cluny museum : *Sight*, the lady is looking at herself in a hand-glass, — *Hearing*, the Lady is singing, with a musical instrument beside her, — *Smell*, the Lady is sniffing the perfume of flowers, — *Taste*, the Lady is eating a fruit while a monkey steals another from a basket, — *Touch*, the Lady is shown caressing a squirrel. It may be, therefore, that this was a fairly frequent theme in mediaeval tapestry, although it seems that no other example is still in existence. Cardinal Erard de la Mark, Prince-Bishop of Liège, possessed a tapestry showing the five senses of man, which was bought from his estate in 1539 by Mencia de Mendoza, under the title *Los Sentidos*. The documents in which it is mentioned unfortunately give no details of their representation.

Thus, there can hardly be any doubt as to the identification of the five Cluny tapestries. *Sight*, is symbolised by the unicorn, observing itself in the hand-glass held out to him by the seated maiden, — *Hearing*, by the sound from the portable organ played by the Lady and worked by her maid-servant, — *Touch*, by the gesture of the maiden holding the unicorn's horn. In the two remaining panels, the symbolism is less obvious : in *Taste*, the Lady is absentmindedly helping herself to a sweet from a comfit-dish, paying little attention to the parakeet perched like a falcon on her wrist. The monkey at her feet is putting something into its mouth, and here the meaning is more clear; one may wonder, on the other hand, what can be the significance of the semi-circular fence covered with climbing roses. As for *Smell*, the girl is merely wreathing a chaplet from a dish of carnations held out by her maidservant, but the monkey, seated on a stool and sniffing the flower he has stolen from the basket, indicates the symbolic meaning of the scene. Five such hypotheses, each backing up the other and converging in the global explanation of the five senses, can be considered as proof.

Design of the tapestry once belonging to Charles de Bourbon, Gaignières collection.

There remains the sixth panel, *A mon seul désir*. At first sight, it hardly seems to fit into the series of tapestries in the Cluny museum. We have pointed that the six panels were considered during the 18th century to be part of the same ensemble. A study of the style, as we shall see, reinforces this theory and leaves no place for the idea, presented by certain commentators, that it is the only surviving remnant of another tapestry. In that case, we should have to suppose that Jean Le Viste had commissioned from the same artist a considerable number of cartoons, so similar that the maiden, the maidservant, the lion, the unicorn and the coats of arms were practically identical. The composition would have always been the same, with a blue « island » against a pink background. All these tapestries would have been executed by weavers of the same establishment, since they show no difference in technique.

It is more probable that *A mon seul désir* does indeed form part of the same series as the *Five Senses*. Kendrick already thought it to be an introduction to this series. Cardinal la Marck's tapestry confirms this hypothesis, since *Los sentidos* also comprised six pieces. The last of them bore the inscription *Liberum arbitrium*, which has the same meaning as that over the tent in our own tapestry : *A mon seul désir*. We know what the philosophers meant by « free will » : for Socrates and Plato it was the natural disposition to behave rightly, which we lose because, through our senses, we become the slaves of our passions. Thus we find the explanation of a scene which has so far been wrongly interpreted. We have always been told that the maiden is choosing a necklace from the casket held out to her by her maidservant. On the contrary, she is carefully replacing it in this casket after having taken it from her neck — she is shown wearing it in the five other panels — and wrapping it in a cloth. It is impossible to give any other interpretation to the gesture with which she is dropping the object from her two hands into the casket, and its significance becomes even more evident in view of the words « *à mon seul désir* », that is, « in accordance only with my will. » The cast-off necklace symbolises the renunciation of the passions aroused by the senses when they are not under control.

Tapestry and armory

An iconographic study of the tapestry cannot be limited solely to an explanation of the subject; the renunciation of slavery to the senses. It must also deal with the armorial aspect which throws light on many obscure points.

First, however, we must say something about the famous unicorn which has earned a world-wide reputation for the Cluny tapestry and given it its name. This fabulous animal was born in the imagination of antiquity and first mentioned by Ctesias, a Greek doctor living at the court of Artaxerxes Mnemon, in about 400 B.C. The body somewhat resembles that of a horse, but with forked hooves and a goat's head surmounted by a long, straight, coiled horn — hence its name : unicorn, *unicornus* — which is in fact the immensely developed upper canine tooth of the narwhal, or cetacean of the arctic seas.

Aristotle and Pliny publicised its image, while during the Middle Ages it became surrounded by a halo of mystery. The unicorn was supposed to have prodigious strength, so that it could be captured only by a young virgin. It appears frequently in mediaeval iconography, especially towards the end of the Middle Ages. In the Cluny museum, we see it on a 15th century leather casket and in the tapestry from the cathedral at Auxerre which recounts the legend of Saint Etienne. In the Cloisters Museum in New York, a series of famous tapestries portrays the Hunting of the Unicorn. A drawing from the Gaignières collection, made from a lost tapestry once belonging to

Charles de Bourbon, shows it in an enclosure, kneeling before a young girl.

The unicorn also plays an important part in the language of heraldry : shown facing another unicorn, or often a lion, as in the arms of England or rearing up along an escutcheon as on armorial supporter. The role of the lion and the unicorn in the Cluny tapestry is somewhat different. In *Smell* and *Taste*, they rear, facing each other and holding flagshafts decorated with silver crescents, on which float the banner and standard of the Le Viste's. They also carry either the armorial escutcheon — that of the lion in *Smell* shows the arms curiously reversed — or a coat of arms worn as a cape over their shoulders — the arms being « twisted » on that of the lion in *Taste*. In *A mon seul désir*, they are shown lifting up the flaps of the tent, and merely presenting the banner and standard. The same is true in the case of *Hearing* except that the animals are not reared up. In *Sight*, only the lion is carrying a banner, while in *Touch* this is born by the Lady, while the lion and the unicorn carry only the armoured escutcheon. Since the unicorn is never shown alone, it would be more exact to speak of « *The Lady with the Lion and the Unicorn* ».

It is not by chance that the arms of the Le Viste's figure so continually and are even portrayed four times in *Smell*, and *Taste*. There were numerous purely armorial tapestries during the Middle Ages — a fact revealed by documents and inventories rather than by the few pieces still in existence — but in no other tapestry did the arms mingle so profusely with the scenes represented. We notice moreover that here the banners and standards are weapons of war, terminating in sharp steel points, and not merely for use at jousts. This leads us to conclude that Jean Le Viste, when he commissioned the tapestry, was being deliberately misleading. He came of a family which was not noble but was trying desperately to become so. Thus he adroitly introduced into these pacific and secular allegories, spears, banners and standards, as if he was a warrior. We might also consider the reason for the tent, surmounted by a small pennant, which greatly resembles the military tents which used to be erected during the 15th century before the ramparts of a town about to be stormed or besieged. It also recalls, however, the tent in the famous miniature of the *Angelical Salutation*, in which duc Philip the Good is seen kneeling before the Virgin, or that in

Painting with the emblematic of Charles de Bourbon in the chapel of the Lyon's cathedral, Gaignières collection.

Lord offering a Heron to a Lady, *Metropolitan Museum, New-York.*

Philip the Good's armorial panel, woven before 1466, Historical Museum, Berne. ▶

a drawing by Gaignières made from a painting by Charles de Bourbon, which also shows standards, flags and spears.

However that may be, *The Lady and the Unicorn*, which must be interpreted at several different levels, certainly testifies to the pretentions of a rapidly ascending middle-class family. Like so many others the Le Viste's had come from the provinces to make their career in the Royal Administration, where they had already acceded to the highest positions. Yet they had still not been ennobled, whereas the Jouvenal's were to become Juvénal des Ursins, and it seems that neither Jean nor Antoine Le Viste ever attained this supreme honour. The Cluny tapestry shows how greatly he desired it, and this desire is echoed in his will, in which he demands to be portrayed in the stained-glass window of his chapel at Vindecy « dressed as a knight, with a coat of mail bearing his arms. » In the same way, this high magistrate had himself proudly described on his funeral slab as Lord of Arcy-sur-Loire.

III. Problems of Style.

It is easy to explain the reputation and wide-spread fame of *The Lady and the Unicorn*. First of all, it is impossible not to be charmed by the range of colouring in each panel. This range comprises only a limited number of tones — always shaded off — to translate the immense variety of elements composing the scene. Yet these limited means suffice to create a magical poetry.

The rounded « island » which serves as the base for the scene, is dark blue, and planted over with tufts of growing flowers, whereas the pink or red background is scattered with flowering branches torn from their trunk. In spite of what is generally sup-

posed, this was not unusual in the Middle Ages. This is testified by certain pieces still in existence, some of them dating from the first third of the 15th century — two inversed copies of *A Knightly Couple* and a *Lady holding a Falcon* in New York; others from the end of the 15th or beginning of the 16th centuries — a *Lord offering a Heron to a Lady* (New York), a *Departure for the Hunt* (Chicago), two *Allegories* (ex-collection Martin-Leroy) and a few others. We learn from documents that the background was not always « ruddy », that is, red, but also white or yellow.

The mille-fleurs planted in the ground relate the tapestry to the plentiful series of tapestries from the end of the Middle Ages, described by the texts as *verdures*. The oldest existing example is Philip the Good's armorial panel in the Historical Museum in Berne, which was executed in Brussels by Jean Le Haze shortly before 1466. It is woven of gold and silver threads and is of the highest quality. Few verdures can be compared with it : most of them are executed somewhat roughly in wool and silk, on cartoons often reutilised, and are rarely the work of highly talented artists. « Flowering branches torn from the tree », on a red background, are found less frequently than « planted tufts » on a dark blue one. Apart from the tapestries already mentioned, we see the former on a green background in the famous *Penelope* in the Boston museum, commissioned by Ferry de Clugny, bishop of Tournai between 1480 and 1483. This unusual décor was perhaps inspired by the custom of strewing the ground with cut flowers on fête days.

In Cluny, this fairyland of flowers is completed by the four trees we see in each panel (except in *Sight*, where there are only two). These are the oak, the pine, the holly and a flowering orange-tree and they may well have some symbolic meaning we cannot fathom. As for the animals portrayed on both the

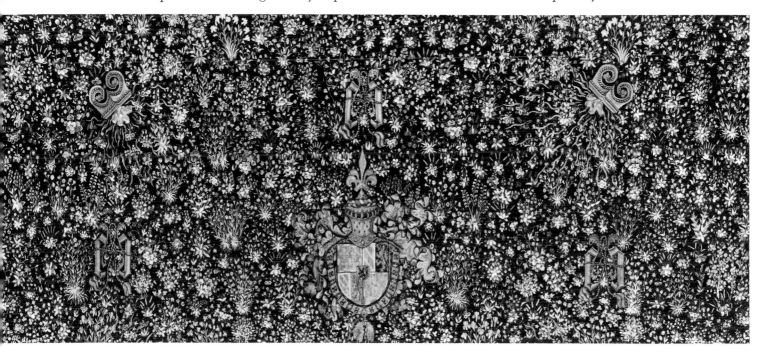

Sight

Hearing

Taste

Smell

Touch

A mon seul désir

◄ Penelope, *Boston Museum.*

73

red and blue backgrounds, these are commonly seen in verdure tapestries, but seldom in such numbers. Here we have a lion-cub, panther, cheetah, wolf, fox, dog, goat, genet, lamb, rabbit, monkey, heron, falcon, magpie, duck and partridge. There is even a young unicorn whose horn is not yet grown (*Taste*) a falcon in flight with shackled wings (*A mon seul désir*) and a monkey attached to a roller (*Touch*).

This marvellous décor emphasises the elegance of the maiden, portrayed six times, in a different attitude and wearing a different costume. This is not, of course, the same personnage repeated six times, since each of these allegorical figures is representative of a different sense. Thus the face is rounder in *Sight* and *Taste*, longer elsewhere, and especially long in *Touch*. The artist has not sought to reproduce the features of any one woman and we must renounce once and for all the theory that these were representations, or even portraits, of Claude Le Viste and her niece Jeanne.

The charm of this proud princess is enhanced by her splendid clothes : shimmering velvets, revealing a glimpse of a magnificent brocaded gown, stamped with abundant pomegranates, wide bands of embroidery, pearls and precious stones around the neckline or bordering the sleeves or slit skirts — all this reveals a love of luxury surely prevalant at the time. The very jewels — diadems, necklaces, clasps, belts, only emphasise such riches without adding to their brilliance. Everywhere we find a striving for variety, and especially in the Lady's headdress : in *Touch*, the hair hangs loose down her back from a heavy, pointed diadem; in *Taste*, it is cut short under a transparent veil held in place by a headband, while in *A mon seul désir* it flows from a thick turban with an aigrette; in *Smell*, it is almost hidden by a short veil falling to the shoulders. Finally, in *Sight* and *Hearing*, it is plaited and tied with ribbons, then twisted into an aigrette above the forehead. This was apparently a fashion of the day, since headdresses of this type are to be seen in the *Penelope* in Boston, and a *Perseus* in a private collection.

The maidservant is dressed more simply but with the same refinement of elegance. The costumes do not appear to be those worn at the French Court. They may have come from Italy, like the materials of which they are made, but they are probably due largely to the painter's imagination.

The model-maker

We must now consider two problems from the history of art which have provoked arguments and even polemics between specialists of tapestry. There are no documents to decide this controversy and we must approach with prudence the two questions : who was the artist who designed *The Lady and the Unicorn?* and, where was it woven?

Three operations are necessary to produce a tapestry : an artist designs the « models », that is, more or less exact compositions on a small scale. A cartoonist transposes these models to the required size, and they become « cartoons ». Finally, weavers reproduce these cartoons, using their own particular weaving techniques. This process naturally becomes less creative at each further stage. It is almost entirely so during the first, the second is merely a question of perfecting certain details; while in the third, it concerns only the choice of colours and of the techniques to be used. During the Middle Ages the relationship between the different corporations concerned was sometimes strained. In 1476, there was a law-suit, followed by an agreement : where verdures were concerned, the cartoonists and weavers were allowed to give free rein to their imagination only in the deliniation of leaves, trees, bushes, flowers and animals. The rest must be left to the painters. This ruling concerned in fact only the city of Brussels and to apply it elsewhere is to risk falling into error. Nevertheless, it is fairly easy to distinguish in the verdures of the late 15th and early 16th centuries between those due to the weavers and cartoonists, who used the same stereotyped effects over and over again, and those which reveal the talent of a painter creating an original work of art.

The composition, the drawing of the personnages and the style of the Cluny tapestry show that it definitely belongs to the second category.

Each scene is admirably balanced, constructed in the form of a pyramid on a vertical axis. In *A mon seul désir*, the tent, with its two open flaps, forms a splendid setting for the maiden; a little dog perched on a stool is symetric to the maidservant, as the lion is to the unicorn. In *Hearing*, it is the hand-organ which creates the axis around which evolve the Lady and her handmaiden. In *Smell*, it is the young woman herself; here, the balance might have been affected by the presence on the left of the maidservant, but it is restored by that on the right of the stool on which perches the mischievous monkey. In *Taste* the axis lies at the centre of the confit-dish. In *Touch*, it is provided by the slender silhouette of the lady herself, while the long horn she touches with her left hand corresponds to the spear in her right, as does the lion to the unicorn's body. The trees reinforce this impression by creating vertical effects in addition to those produced by the banners and standards. These lines do more than create a rhythm. Starting at different levels, they produce an effect of perspective, with the vanishing point on a level with the spectator's eye. This is especially evident in *Sight*, *Taste* an *A mon seul désir*. Then, in order to avoid a risk of monotony, the composition of *Touch* centres on a

Departure for the Hunt, *mille-fleurs tapestry, first series, Metropolitan Museum, New-York.* ▶

diagonal passing through the unicorn's horn and the spear, up to the tip of the pine-tree on the left. In *Hearing*, the effect of depth is obtained by means of the diagonal perspective of the table on which stands the portable organ, this perspective being repeated to the right by the unicorn's horn and the pine-tree.

This evident intention to create an impression of depth is emphasised by the oval form of the « island », which is more or less tilted in the different panels. Thus the composition of each scene reveals the work of a great artist who knew that the blue base, seen in perspective, would contrast with the pink background closing the composition.

Scholars have attempted to identify the painter who created the six models. Mme Reynaud recently tried to attribute them to one of the pupils of Henri and Conrad de Vulcop whose whole artistic production she has grouped together. According to her, this artist, whom she calls the « Master of Anne de Bretagne », inherited a number of their models and made considerable use of these. Thus she believes him to be responsible for the models of the most famous tapestries of the end of the century : *Perseus* (private collection), *Illustrious Women* with *Penelope* (Boston), *Life of the Virgin* from the cathedral of Bayeux, the Cluny tapestry, and above all the famous tapestries in the Cloisters Museum representing *The Hunting of the Unicorn*. Mme Souchal has repeated and amplified these conclusions in her study of this artist, whom she names « The Master of the Hunting of the Unicorn ». She attributes to him numerous contemporary engravings, including some magnificent woodcuts, stained-glass windows and the above-mentioned tapestries. This list includes in fact the whole artistic production in Paris during the last twenty years of the 15th century and the first ten of the 16th. It is hard to believe that one man of however varied and multiple talents, could produce so much. It is impossible here to reconsider this question in general and we can only take account of the comparisons established between the tapestries of the Cloisters Museum and those of Cluny. We have remarked elsewhere that the American tapestries belong to three different ensembles : a mille-fleurs, with the *Departure for the Hunt* and the living unicorn imprisoned in an enclosure; the second, comprising four panels, portraying the hunt, the kill, and the transport of the massacred animal; and finally, a last, separate panel from a different series shows the capture by a young girl of the unicorn pursued by hounds (cf. the frontispiece to this study). Since each of these three series shows distinctive features, we cannot be sure they are the work of the same model-maker, nor does it necessarily follows from comparisons supposedly established between the *Capture by a*

◄ The Kill of the Unicorn, *mille-fleurs tapestry, second series, Metropolitan Museum, New-York.*

Young Girl tapestry and the *Lady and the Unicorn*, that the other six panels are by the same artist. Furthermore, when the tapestries from Cluny and the Cloisters Museum were shown together at the exhibition held at the Grand Palais in Paris, then in the Metropolitan Museum in New York, the stylistic resemblances were not apparent. The differences, on the contrary, became evident. They appeared on several planes : on the technical plane, since in New York we see gold and silver thread used in profusion, whereas in Paris the thread is of wool or silk. Then, in the style : the resemblances detected are due to the spirit of the period rather than the hand of the same artist. This interesting but hazardous attempt to identify the model-maker of the *Lady and the Unicorn* has the merit of pointing out that he was trained as an artist in Paris or in Court circles, and executed his designs there. This conclusion is not surprising when we recall that Jean Le Viste, who lived for a time in the Sancerre mansion on the Quai des Augustins in Paris, made his career in the capital.

The second question which has not been satisfactorily answered concerns the place where the *Lady and the Unicorn* was woven. We can ignore the claims of the workshops in the province of La Marche — Aubusson and Felletin — which did not yet exist at the end of the 15th century : they were upheld for a time simply because of the presence of the tapestry at Boussac, where it arrived only in the 17th century.

More recently, it was thought that all the « mille-fleurs » were executed by itinerant workshops travelling in the Loire district, going from château to château according to the orders received. This idea was born simply because many of these tapestries are to be found in that part of the country, or originate from it. There is no documentary evidence of any activity of this sort, so it was even suggested that these nomadic workmen left no archives. This theory has not withstood the test of history : new texts have revealed the immense production of « verdures » in the northern districts. The history of economics has thrown light on the history of art : the decline of the cloth industry in the Burgundian Netherlands had begun in the 14th century and left thousands of unemployed. The Dukes of Burgundy were anxious to utilise for the benefit of their States the abundant capital, qualified manpower and expert dyers available and it was they who encouraged and supported an inevitable reconversion. This took the form of tapestry, the technique of which was not unlike that of cloth-making and the fabrication of various materials. This activity, born out of special economic conditions, produced an impressive number of masterpieces.

According to Mrs Schneebalg-Perelman, there is documentary evidence of some five hundred tapestry-workers in Brussels — a figure which becomes explicable in the light of the above-mentioned circumstances. It is possible to follow the ascent in Brussels of this new corporation, which became independant in 1447 and came into conflict with that of the painters in 1476. Brussels, however, was not the only northern city with an intensive production. There are no statistics to show the relative importance of Brussels, Ghent, Audenarde or Arras. It seems now that Lille was more productive than has been supposed, and Tournai much less. Antwerp and Bruges were then international ports and thanks to them and to the branches of the Medicis Bank set up in the countries of the North, this huge production could be easily circulated throughout the whole of western Europe. In this way, new capital flowed, in making possible new investments.

There have been attemps to distinguish, either by their techniques or through a stylistic analysis, between the production of the different centres, since it was thought that each city had its own methods. This proved to be impossible except where an attribution was based on some really convincing text. Who would have thought that the tapestry of *St. Anatoile of Salins* had been woven in Bruges if there had been no documents to prove it? Or that the tapestry in Montacute House figuring Jean de Daillon hails from Tournai?

The affair is further complicated now we know that weavers travelled between the different centres, either for their own pleasure or according to the fluctuations of the market. Nor should we forget that heads of workshops did not hesitate to sub-contract when they suddenly found themselves with too many orders on their hands. Thus it seems illusory to claim that a production comes from this or that city. Furthermore, we are told that the weavers had no say in questions of style, which was imposed solely by the model or cartoon. We know many examples of models executed elsewhere and sent to be woven in the Flemish centres. This must have been so in the case of *The Lady and the Unicorn*, the designs for which were made by a Parisian artist and sent to be carried out in some northern city.

Mrs Schneebalg-Perelman emphasises on the one hand the role played by Brussels in the 14th century, and on the other, the fact that one of the finest mille-fleurs of the end of the 14th century (the tapestry with the arms of Philip the Good) was woven there, and concludes from this that the same was true in the case of *The Lady and the Unicorn*. This theory is not impossible, but cannot be considered as a certainly since there is no text to prove it.

We should also remark that the weaver or weavers who wove the six panels were not always as skilful as the authors of the models and cartoons. How, otherwise, can we explain the clumsy hands of the young girl and the badly-drawn face of the servant in *Hearing*; or the girls slightly twisted mouth in *Touch?* The beauty of the Cluny tapestry is not lessened by these undeniable blunders; in general, the details are rendered with the greatest delicacy. Jean Le Viste, the model-maker, the painter of the cartoons, and the weavers used all their ingenuity to produce a work which enchants us by its deep significance, the beauty of the draftsmanship and the charm of its colours.

In conclusion, we must admit that the Cluny tapestry forms a complete series illustrating the five senses, with a panel to introduce or conclude it, portraying the renunciation of all passion. It was certainly not a wedding present. It bears witness, on the contrary, to the glory of a member of the Le Viste family. In view of the date of its execution, it must have been commissioned by Jean Le Viste, who also ordered other tapestries with a pink background, which have now disappeared. The date has been established as being between 1484 and 1500. Two questions remain unanswered : the name of the artist who produced the models, and the place where the tapestry was woven.

Alain Erlande-Brandenburg.

The design and lay-out of this volume
devoted to the tapestries of « the Lady and the Unicorn »,
are due to Pierre Faucheux.
The type was set up at Baskerville
and the edition was completed on July 22, 1983
by the Union Press in Paris
for the Union of the National Museums of France.
The photographs are due to the Photographic
Department of the Union of the National Museums,
89 avenue Victor Hugo, 75116 Paris.